*The
Company
of
Heaven*

Also by Jeffrey Skinner

POETRY
Late Stars, 1985
A Guide to Forgetting, 1988
The Night Lifted Us (with Sarah Gorham), 1991

PROSE
Real Toads in Imaginary Gardens (with Stephen Policoff), 1991

The Company of Heaven

JEFFREY SKINNER

University of Pittsburgh Press
Pittsburgh • London

The publication of this book is supported by grants from the National Endowment for the Arts in Washington, D.C., a Federal agency, and the Pennsylvania Council on the Arts.

Published by the University of Pittsburgh Press, Pittsburgh, Pa. 15260
Copyright © 1992, Jeffrey Skinner
All rights reserved
Manufactured in the United States of America
Printed on acid-free paper

Library of Congress Cataloging-in-Publication Data

Skinner, Jeffrey.
   The company of heaven / Jeffrey Skinner.
     p. cm.—(Pitt poetry series)
   ISBN 0-8229-3721-2 (alk. paper).—ISBN 0-8229-5481-8 (pbk. : alk. paper)
    I. Title. II. Series.
PS3569.K498C66   1992
811'.54—dc20   92-50196
                                                                                                                         CIP

A CIP catalogue record for this book is available from the British Library. Eurospan, London

The author and publisher wish to express their grateful acknowledgment to the following publications in which some of these poems first appeared: *Always a River* ("Unable to Pack the River, You Leave It Behind"); *Art/Life* ("Animal Discount," "Invitation to the Dreamer," "The New Days"); *The Atlantic Monthly* ("Carver," "For Stuart Porter, Who Asked for a Poem That Would Not Depress Him Further"); *Confrontation* ("Salt Marsh Cordgrass"); *Crosscurrents* ("Thanksgiving Over the Water"); *Cumberland Poetry Journal* ("Girl In a Dogwood Tree," formerly "Young Girl In a Dogwood Tree"); *Cutbank* ("Shore Report"); *Ironwood* ("Bajo Cruces y Espadas," "Echo Off"); *The Louisville Review* ("Inversion," "Mermaid's Purse"); *Ohio Review* ("The Delicates," "Late Afternoon, Late in the Twentieth Century"); *Poetry* ("The Company of Heaven," "The Dangerous Teaching," "Like Water," "Living Poets," "Those Who Insist They've Returned"); *Poetry East* ("All Saints," "Questionable Weather"); *Raccoon* ("The Visible Man"); *The Southern Poetry Review* ("Mark, Fore & Strike"); *The Southern Review* ("The Ocean All Day, All Night"); and *Yellow Silk* ("Silk Robe," "Young Woman Getting Ready for Work").

The poem, "For Stuart Porter, Who Asked for a Poem That Would Not Depress Him Further," was reprinted in *America* and *Stardate*. "Calm Evening" was awarded the 1991 Cecil Hemley Memorial Award from the Poetry Society of America.

The author would like to thank the National Endowment for the Arts and the Delaware State Arts Council for their generous support, and Dick Allen and Tom Byers for help with the manuscript.

for Sarah

Contents

I. The Company of Heaven
Like Water *3*
The Company of Heaven *4*
For Stuart Porter, Who Asked for a Poem That Would Not Depress
    Him Further *9*
Those Who Insist They've Returned *10*
The Delicates *12*
Earth Angel *13*
Living Poets *15*
Carver *17*
Late Afternoon, Late in the Twentieth Century *18*

II. Unable to Pack the River
Young Woman Getting Ready for Work *23*
Mark, Fore & Strike *24*
The Visible Man *26*
The New Days *30*
The Day in the Window *31*
The Dangerous Teaching *32*
Girl in a Dogwood Tree *34*
Calm Evening *35*
Unable to Pack the River, You Leave It Behind *38*

III. Animal Discount
Bajo Cruces y Espadas *45*
Fable of the Knife *46*
Animal Discount *47*
Objects in Mirror Are Closer Than They Appear *48*
Questionable Weather *49*
Shore Report *50*

Silk Robe *52*
Restoration *53*
Inversion *55*
Echo Off *56*

IV. Thanksgiving Over the Water
Invitation to the Dreamer *59*
Thanksgiving Over the Water *60*
Lacrimae Patris *61*
Mermaid's Purse *63*
All Saints *64*
Salt Marsh Cordgrass *65*
The Starling Migration *66*
The Ocean All Day, All Night *68*
The Moment When the Workers of the Night Pass by the Workers of the Day *69*

I. The Company of Heaven

Like Water

The oldest souls prefer Ireland and Africa,
turning as every soul does in the end to green
or beige, cormorant and ibis.
They have no fingers, of course, but the idea
of fingers is important to them, they
wear the idea like a bone necklace. They live on
great quantities of sea air or the explosive
atmosphere inside grain elevators, can feed
anywhere humans have been working—
they love to drift in the tart air
of a garage empty and black as oil rags
all night. But generally they move like candles
in a snowfall in the woods. The young ones
are filled with crude desire and will leap in
to any life, even short ones bound for murder
or dismemberment; the young ones
are hungry, their edges sharp as glass.
All of them whisper, sing, are saddened
by memory like us. That is why they must return.
Like ice, their time in this state is brief.
And whether soul finds body or body
finds soul is never clear. But once the match
is made the soul pours in, like water,
taking the shape of whatever it fills.

The Company of Heaven

1

Those who have risen
and those who remain attached, how similar their faces
in certain hours of light! A young couple

invite the new priest to dinner
and the husband is relieved to see him smoke and drink,
even swear mildly from the lawn chair

as the sun dips an edge in the bay
and the horizon hisses up with a light
that is the ancient marriage of lion and rose.

2

And the man with ruined legs
so hard not to avoid
there every Sunday in a summer cotton shirt
and black jeans
handlebar mustache and a tongue
clumsy as a thumb,
how many have seen him how many times
trying to pick up young girls
near the pizza booth
in the mall?

The head steward, on the other hand, is a handsome
man.

Who can afford the poor.

3

Always seems to swelter at the annual picnic,
beer and volleyball on the church lawn,
children playing hide-and-seek in the enwrapping grave-
yard, their fingers leaving thin trails of moisture
on the cool stones

in the vertical light of noon
when dogs trot the sidewalks like marines on drill
tongues jabbing the air
alert for a puddle or a place to lie down,
serrated patch of grass, shade . . .
                                    Listen,

if you let the deepest question enter you
it will emerge, not as words
but simplest elements: salt, water.

4

Under the bank clock on Second Street,
under a sky without a moon
without a visible moon
only the quiet of streetlamp hum
and the sound when the temperature changes
to time, like the turning of a page
in a metal book,

now that we read time in pulses of light
and have the formula for thin layers
of ceramic with zero
resistance to electricity,

now that the tree
outside my window turns to waken
the green sleep
holding its branches out to the poor
side of town, like Joshua,
full of birds and their carousel music, now.

5

And the older couple with faces moving
into the dark, they push brochures
on us full of green lawns and
tailored mountains,
he passes the brass plate up and down
the aisle,
she shines near the dark with the joy
of second marriage late in life, saying

Spring presses against my will and I flower

I release my children like beams of light . . .

6

If the sun should wander through God's mind
still it is only an average star.

Trouble knows the congregation
and they diminish, flowers on the altar.

The church faces east and when the last
hymn is sung the priest flings open

the doors to the scent of the Atlantic,
clean and gray as the inside of a cloud.

7

And an angel appeared before us once
        he could have done any work he wanted
of course, or none
        but chose to clean fish down at the docks
and live in a one-room apartment
on the black side of town (no one
        seems to remember if he was a black
        angel or a white angel) quiet

as he walked we could tell he was
an angel by the way he sang the descant
        so pure his voice made the chalice ring
and one Sunday was gone, simply

and when his apartment was opened

        the landlord found the walls, ceiling,
the couch and every square inch of
                      surface

covered with fish scales, shining iridescent.

8

On the parish-hall bulletin board
      picture of a smiling Ethiopian child
and sign-up sheet for spaghetti dinner
           we will attend
seeking salvation among fellow creatures
      of bread and wine
                  dreamer
during the sermon
clouds cast a moving shadow
across the tall colored windows
      and the light brightens
then fades like the wafer
      melting on the roof of my mouth

And those who won't pray also believe
turning to each other, turning
           to the mountains and lakes, *kyrie*

eleison they start singing
in their way when the sparrows finish . . .

Oh faith, you are so shy and eager to please
like a homely child,
like the room inside the mirror,

it is difficult to believe
you can hold such angels and arch-
angels, all

the company of heaven. . . .

8

For Stuart Porter, Who Asked for a Poem That Would Not Depress Him Further

A joke the size of a small moon headed
for earth: it will decimate all talk of aging
schedules and quarterly projections. The dictators
will laugh themselves to death,
the crippled shall walk and the blind see.
Every heart shall open like rain
and the rivers flow
with gladness, oh my brother . . . I'm making
this up, of course, but you get the point—
imagination is a means of transport,
sometimes more real than any other, and I can see
you reading now, the smile beginning,
the corners of your lips raised,
slightly. And sometimes it's enough, a belly laugh's
redundant, the small
pleasure we can hold expands, takes up whole
moments of our lives. I think of your daughter
lying peaceful on the couch
in your lonely condo, her face like a perfected dream
of your own, translated into the feminine,
how your hands took on
a sudden grace I'd never seen
when you lifted her, turned her away
from the harsh light . . . It's coming! The astronomers
are already beginning to snicker! Close all doors
and windows, hustle to the cellar!
—How could we bear total joy when one small
speechless face transforms
our hearts, all our wounds forever-after bathed
in the light of that gaze so fresh from the other world. . . .

Those Who Insist They've Returned

for Gail Gorham

What is this light they always bring up, rising
above the teetering body? What is the eye
set free? Why not a vision of descent
for a change, a few daydreams of the star-

nosed mole, or some sweaty earthbound hack
through vegetation? That I could swallow.
But, no, always they float over the steel table
noting with remarkable accuracy

which tube the doctor inserts where and when,
every word spoken, each hard punch to the chest;
calm, detached, their airy bags packed
and ready to leave. Then why do they return?

There they are, just on the verge of tearful embrace
with the resurrected dead of their own lives,
all smiling and glowing with knowing comfort—
celestial welcoming party—only to be called back

down a sweet tunnel into the body in time,
reviving then, choking a little, looking up
at the masked people in green. Then out
through hallways that stink with covered food

into the world of volume. On TV, they grin
like happy idiots as they tell the story;
they seem to think that *now* they will live
forever. Go figure. The rest of us look for

a way to rise outside of death, shackled
to contention, to the face falling steadily
in the mirror. You know what I'm saying.
There are as many kinds of death as creatures

to die, and surely it is entrance. But
what is loosed here shall be loosed in heaven,
and whatever light we manage here, what love,
like a beam in black space, will accompany us out.

The Delicates

You must bow down to hear the complaint
of dust, the dry cough of nonbeing.
You have to rise up to see the nude in the mirror
as other, as a man who has just eaten dinner
and will soon sleep. So it is vertical—
the current moves between feet and moon, the sun
rises, traffic rants. There is so much to be done!

. . . Later that same day a cool drink pauses
on the veranda, and the man hesitates at the rusted
shed door, hearing things. A gentle grunting.
This is not a good time for chasing beasts:
twilight, just before the soup is served, when
deer and the other delicates tiptoe to the pond,
when we hunger, and the soul is most liable to rise.

Earth Angel

Mica, if you peel carefully,
comes off in thin, clear panes,
lenses to see the angel. In my seventh year
I kept rocks in egg cartons, one
rock to replace each egg, and the angel
would sit at my elbow, still
as a diamond or the blue heart
of flame. He was a collector
too, and when I showed him my stamps,
the faces and flags embossed,
the tenderness of pastel greens,
reds and yellows, he danced
all whirl and elbows in the air
and a hay-scented breeze poured
from his sleeves. This was the year
satellites learned the word *orbit*
and the stars quivered in my telescope,
the angel impatient for his turn.
This was the year I showed
my father's gun to Ronnie (the angel,
not knowing what to feel, hovered
inside the willow); Ronnie
held the gun, his eyes fastened
to it, though the firing pin
had been removed, and was impressed,
was my friend. This was the
year Frankie Dunn blew off part
of his pinkie with a cherry bomb,
and the angel dragged me inside
where we watched the street
from the attic, the sparks flying
up from the dark as if the earth
were flint struck by invisible
steel. This was the year I remember
hiding in a circle of lilac

bushes, and the rain beginning
then, and the happiness of rain
in the smell of lilacs . . . This was
the year I woke up to the self
as history, and all the childish
forces took on names, and rocks
in the carton became quartz, schist,
pyrite, iron slag, limestone,
anthracite and mica. And the song,
Earth Angel, became a hit,
transistors bloomed on every pillow
and the angel went out into the world.

Living Poets

for Michael Collier

In a sense we are trying to please our readers,
offering them grief, candy, vistas, and sex.
And in a sense we have no readers. Strange,
to be here so intensely, even in the mall

where I am touched by the harried blond
mother with three kids and a tattoo on her bicep.
Strange that in an odd second I can say that
and love her, then walk out and forget her.

And her children, of course. Chances are they'll
amount to nothing, though now they entreat
with such passion, they argue with unwrapped
genius for french fries and CDs. Most of us

live and die, small smudges in the immediate
family, the local history, but you couldn't
have sold me that idea in my twenties!
I thought we were all going to live forever!

I'm nervous about my poet friends, and me.
We write so well our lines may lift
into a thick paste of clouds, but that woman
stuffing hot dogs into three miniature faces,

what poem could change her life? She'll never
read a poem, is the answer. Give us this
day, is the answer. Poetry's past care or change,
that's the answer, and the problem. That woman

wants baked ham for Sunday, a new lunch-
box for the middle girl; maybe, if the bonus
comes, a weekend at the shore with her husband, alone.
How can we compete
      with such intimate desires?

Carver

There was no landscape so hard
he could not return
with its poetry.

And there it was—the champagne
hidden in the bathroom,
the blocked ear, the peacock

strutting through
the laborer's dining room;
everything we had missed

out of self-regard
or loftiness. People who die
in the stories die simply,

for no point, and those left
can only comfort
not turn away. Now the teacher

leaves the room, and the students
hush under the loud clock.
Whatever they can see

through the window,
the flat earth too poor and dry
for growing, they are on their own.

Late Afternoon,
Late in the Twentieth Century

Dusk in Creason's Park comes on slow,
darkening the folds in the children's jackets,
the fall air beer-colored, thick
as remembrance, and the climbed trees shiver
down last leaves. I try to watch both kids
at once, though they tend to drift
from one steel-and-colored-plastic
jerryrig of slides, bridges and swings,
to another, independent, drawn to separate
peers, and I have to call them back
into one field of vision. There are other
parents here, sitting on the sawhorse
picnic benches, talking or smoking, their
arms spread the table's length, their legs
straight out. One man in his fifties
sits alone, an open briefcase before him,
making notes on a legal pad; office
alfresco . . . It is close to finished,
this century. Soon the 1 will change
to a simple 2, like a circuit changing
its mind from yes to no, like the short
step of a wounded soldier. We have filled
the universe with blood again, to no
one's surprise. And by the river's edge
we complained of thirst, we eyed
the forests and filled them with glare.
We said this edge will fit that space
and it did—the concrete oozed through
wooden forms, a thousand blank faces
rose above us, and we were happy
as a smooth surface, as a just-shot
arrow. We ridiculed the old questions,
stabbing our fingers in their leather chests

until they'd had enough, and headed back
to the salt caverns. We found love shivering
in a bus station and took her home,
tenderly sponging off the superficial
wounds. We gave her tea before the fire.
When she grew old we sold the company
and put her back on the bus. We died,
and the others were outraged, they pounded
fists, they petitioned, they did everything
but join us. Then they joined us. We
starved language, until the bones showed
through and the head dropped off
and rolled away, laughing like an idiot . . .
The dusk in Creason's Park comes on, slowly,
and the parents reel their children in
on the soft hook of their names, and they all
drift toward their cars and thoughts
of food and sleep. *Girls,* I yell, *let's
go!* and they come, breathless and glazed
from play. In them I am well pleased,
and would build a city for their future.
But I will not take credit for their failures.
Lord, they are close to me as my skin
and I snarl when the dress is torn, when
the milk spills. Hear me. I am still that lost.

II. Unable to Pack the River

Young Woman Getting Ready for Work

We all begin in ecstasy, in detail,
it cannot be faked. A pink comb
glows faintly in the same mirror
that holds a woman's breasts,

contains them, somehow.
She needs to get ready for work;
her hair is fine, the comb falls through it
like a slide guitar. I work

the second shift, and on my first
round I lock doors, turn off
machines and lights—I put the moaning
factory to sleep. Mornings I lie

watching her clip a gold hoop
to each ear, brush blue dust, wing
powder, over her eyelids, pull on panties
and the second skin of nylon. She

is happy with her pretty face,
and kisses me as if this will go on.
Drifting off, I hear the latch shut
and, faint in the lower apartment,

our landlord singing in Portuguese.
I dream her nipples
touched by a faceless man. This
will be the day I write my first

poem on the blunt distance in marriage,
at a desk in the factory basement.
The sun on my face wakes me.
It's 1976. I have everything to learn.

Mark, Fore & Strike

In my college town
a men's store—
madras pants, canvas
belts with embossed ducks
or golf clubs repeated,
Oxford shirts. They kept
the shirts in drawers
and it was like rummaging
in Gatsby's bedroom—pastel
blue, pink, and yellow, cotton;
the tight weave, when
you looked closely,
a blend of white and color.
I went to school in Florida
and the shirts, I thought,
were like Florida,
at once passionate
and washed out. All my friends
were thinking like mad
of a way to get out
of the draft: Peter
ate nothing but bananas
and slipped beneath the weight;
Roger went to his physical
on speed, his eyes
acidic dots, willing to stop
at nothing; Rick
closed the door of his van
on his knee, every
morning before class.
I went to bone doctors,
talked a dentist
into reapplying braces,
looked at brochures of neutral
countries. I acted

in the theater and got lousy
grades; a few of us went
and died. Jordan came back
paralyzed from the neck down.
He hung around town
for a year, torturing
his girlfriend and the rest
of us with pity, and guilt.
He'd been a terrific
actor (Hamlet with a lisp)
so we took it. But probably
we would have taken it
if he'd been ungifted,
a jerk . . .

                          This poem
has gotten away from me,
I know, what sometimes happens
when you speak of memory.

Look, I don't know
any of them anymore—
my *peace and love* generation
has vanished into just
people living, trying to live
like anyone before them.
We never would have guessed . . .
The last of those shirts was blue
and I wore it until
two years ago, when
my second daughter was born
and the family moved to another state,
and the collar frayed
beyond mending.

The Visible Man

for Michael Waters

1

The skin transparent, we must imagine
vein, muscle, ligament, the layers of fat
until we reach the long bones of the arms and legs
coupled by staples, white as baby teeth
lying in the fallows of the plastic mold.
The organs must be painted and glued
together, then arranged in the chest cavity,
pieces of a gory puzzle. No, say "learning
toy . . ." His brain, smaller than a walnut,
a bit too small for the skull, rattles
when he's shaken by the legs. After rib cage
comes breastplate, and then he is ready
to stand with night-light and dinosaur,
tilted slightly forward on his platform.

2

Once I had an alcoholic client
who cleared his calendar each time we lunched
and sailed through five Manhattans on the strength
of his bluster—Hitler and the Jews,
ergonomics and the poor at heart. His scalp itched,
he was fat and married three times and wholly
unprejudiced—"I hate everybody."
One day when I dropped in on a routine call
he wasn't there. A blond woman in a wool suit
greeted me in his office. After asking what

I took in my coffee she explained
MacCarron was no longer with the company
and she would be assuming his duties.
That was his name—MacCarron.

3

Sometimes during meditation the eyes tear.
This is a sign of some progress, though
like all other thoughts, visions,
flashing pictures of genitalia,
intimations of divinity
and pain it must be given
no attention. Only refocus
on the breath—in, out, mind in belly . . .
My stay at the monastery was brief,
a flash of robes and dark wood, and when the master
said *The desk is just a desk, the bowl
only a bowl,* I took him at his word . . .
The spiritual life: monotonous
and inexhaustible, even unto death.

4

McCarron calls me at three
in the morning. "Wake up, dick face. When
you gonna take over the business?"
With a slack hold on my own consciousness
I tell him to go fuck himself, let me
sleep, for Christ's sake. But this is a client
so I make it a joke, my forehead pressed to my palm.
Where does he get the energy!

Years later, some guy in a bar tells me
McCarron's third wife left him and he
tried and failed in dry cleaning, now
sits home drinking, phoning the occasional whore
in, his satellite dish whirring in the dark,
rummaging the sky for a dose of Finnish porn.

5

There was a period when he came to life
each night, and I had to will myself awake
or suffer as a dreaming child. You can imagine.
I'd ease myself from the top bunk in the dark
and look with my fingers for the base
of his platform on the top shelf. Some nights
even laying him in a drawer would not remove
his vision: walking toward me with stiff legs,
his organs wet and glistening like fish,
heart beating and the brain glowing faintly;
no speech, only the face drawn down
in supplication and the arms out to his
sides, as if in a shrug, the palms open to me
and the hands that held nothing but bone . . .

6

A field of starlings swirls up in blue air
like pepper stirred into a glass of water.
Driving over flat land: *if you meet the Buddha
on the road, kill him* . . . And it could be anyone!
The black attendant who pumps my gas without a word,

his mind elsewhere; the overweight counselor
in the unemployment office, pushing her glasses
up with a plump index; the cop; the priest;
my own children, who leap on my body like rabbits . . .
It was years ago, two hundred miles away,
almost another life: MacCarron. Somehow he traced
my number, and called, dead-drunk—"I found you,
you son of a bitch, I found you!" his image
coming back, his heart still on his sleeve . . .

The New Days

Childhood is the only country
where we completely understand the language—
a small enclosure of lilac bushes, the smell of
freshly toweled hair, sand in shoe. At the beach
twin concrete towers you can climb
to get a more godlike view of the waves
and the bodies in various stages of collapse . . .
But at this moment my daughter yammers on
in the next room, the primary colors
of her subspeech lending the air
that "light and festive feeling." Somewhere else
tremendous issues rise and contend,
but the tickets are expensive, they cost
like sin—we would have to give up everything.
And then there's no guarantee
it's not all just talk. These days
the forecast changes more rapidly than in
the old days, though weather recalled, fondly, with a few
scattered regrets, seems to matter more,
has a thickness the new days lack.
And the prevailing mood is not sadness
nor anything so elegant
and well-dressed as despair, but a kind of targetless
remorse—we are confused and sorry
and neither ocean nor child nor anything
in between will accept our apologies. My daughter
is getting heavy, I can't carry her
on one arm for hours
as I could in the old days. I put her
down and she starts spinning through the house,
a little world gathering the weight of her new
past, no baby, on the verge of speech.

The Day in the Window

It should be enough, sweet net of family,
each of us caught happily, I think
and lean down to smell the baby's hair—
blond tang of a small mammal. And the way
we have our way with the world,
not often, naturally, but whole moments
when the door stays open and we are seen,
backlit, undeniable. The day in the window,
bright and clear, looks warm, though it may
be cold just beyond the glass. It may be
we will walk out without coats into
a grave mistake, and the old anguish
snow down like ash from a distant
explosion. It may be pain is mere destiny.
But even the most graceful child cannot run
with a full glass of water and not spill
half, or most, as the mind cannot hold
every possibility. Always, the one loss
more. This is why Kannon, though she could
have shed her body like a bulky coat
and vanished into pure freedom, chose
to stay, changing the bandages of the wounded.
Later, I think we'll all walk downtown,
the four of us, holding Laura's hand,
Bonnie in the stroller. And if it's not
too cold we'll go down to the Cape Channel,
to the docks where the boats rock
gently in their bays, made fast but
with slack enough, in case the water
shifts, as it does twice a day, ropes
sighing as they're tightened by the moon.

The Dangerous Teaching

All morning I pitch the invisible
to people half my age. I say this table's real, yes,
but once it was an idea of a table, the invisible

is its mother, knocking first on veneer,
then on my temple. Then I stand up grandly
and squeeze a piece of chalk in my fist. You

recall, perhaps, the tin box full of buttons,
every kind of button—glass, lead, leather, stone,
a dozen grades of plastic in a paint box

of colors, how they clicked and spilled through
your hands. Or the nail driven crudely into the side
of the garage, the fleck of dried blood on its head;

what was it for? It was, you'll recall, a cloudy day.
And there, in the cellar rec room, on the clumsy
sofa, it was your first time, over before

you knew it, the blood burning in your hands,
blood burning under the entire skin of you. Or the night
you walked from Grant's Tomb to the Battery, all night,

until a pink light stained the fog, and you swore if you never
left that place it wouldn't matter.
But it's more than memory, memory is the echo of the once

seen, I'm talking about the never seen, I say,
and sit back down. And finish the last of my coffee,
which has gone cold. The constellations

are dressing up this very moment, I say, on the other
side of the world, with palm trees for earrings
and the silver skid mark of the moon

parting their hair. Oh children, I say, do you
believe? And they rise, and shuffle, and turn
gratefully to the door, leaving for answer

the fresh, shampoo scent of their absence.

Girl in a Dogwood Tree

What is now but increased longing
purified of romance?
Girl, hold on to those branches
that have already dropped their white-
skin petals, red-notched stigmata
of early spring. If you fall
the ground may not forgive you,
may not give. Once I climbed
a pine much too high, up through
a dense whorl of branches
each sticky with its clear blood.
At the top, wind brushed by
my face like a stream of feathers;
I looked down, once, then out
at the red brick mansion,
the rich ones drinking on the lawn.
If I were a man, I thought,
I would not be here,
but I would not be there either.
Or perhaps I thought no
such thing, only climbed down
carefully, my naked arms
and legs cut anyway, quick red lines
the branches drew, hands
sticky with sap. How long
time withholds its coy answer,
then whispers it in a rush,
wind, invisible voice—
telling us through the pores.
Girl, the scent of the future is on my hands,
no washing will quiet it.

Calm Evening

Say God is in a room and on his table he has some cookies and tea, and he's dreaming this whole universe up. Well, we can't reach out and get his cookies. They're not in our universe. See, our universe has bounds. There are some things in it and some things not.

—Edward Fredkin

For a time we flare *yes,*
and *on,* then the wave passes
into other form. My daughters ride circles
on the porch and the death of March
is gentle, a light jacket passing.
I turn sausage on the grill, fat
spits fire in the coals and
smoke ascends suburban heaven.
Lord of the universe, you
are a calm evening, you dream
wind smooth as my daughters' skin,
here, at least, now. Their contention,
the pinches, the pulled hair,
the smacks and pushes, must have
its own necessity, must be part
of the working out; if only the
question could be raised
to perfection . . . Sarah calls
Five minutes from the kitchen
window. Her voice has picked up color,
gold and russet, since we first met,
and where that early lighter voice
has gone, I don't know. But now
is not last night, when I did
the things I claim I'm doing
now, earlier in this poem—

these paper deeds, paper daughters,
my wife's paper voice. Now
I'm just waiting for the mail,
computer humming like a small plane.
Then Laura pushed Bonnie
off her bike—I watched her slow
motion fall from my post at
the grill, her drift into the sorrow
of the world; her wail into my arms
deafened one ear. When she had calmed
to soft sobs I promised two cookies
after dinner, and her tears
joined the past. All our tears
are joined in the past; it is possible
we will never cry again . . . Later,
after dinner, after the girls
had been read to and kissed
off toward sleep, I went out alone
on the porch. Venus hung plumb
beneath the moon, the air so clear
I could see the cold roundness of each
star, and rooftops etched black
against purple sky. The old feeling
of some background beyond good
and evil was in that air
and in me, the ostinato from which
we issue as melody. But that's
too grand—I was just standing
on the porch, glad to be alive,
a bit nostalgic for my youth,
which I could also see in the sky,
in the way I can see God's snack
traveling toward his mouth.

I can reach out and try to touch
it, but I know he'll just
press my hand back into his forehead
gently, gently. And now
the mail still hasn't come, and I
am impatient to get to the rest
of the day. I wonder when I will die.

Unable to Pack the River, You Leave It Behind

for Aleda Shirley

1

I did not ask to be born!
you insist
over cigarettes and iced tea
shaking your black hair wild to make the point.
We sit facing a glass
rectangle,
the view you are leaving.

Wright loved any river
but this one he loved most
because his Jenny bathed here
because he wept first
and longest
at its wracked edges.

I say you did ask
to be born.
I do not say it was an unsorrowful request.

2

Riparian lawn slopes to a steep bank
inlaid with stone,
an iron staircase down to an iron platform
where brown water bobs in the perforations.
My kids throw sticks in the current.
I watch, stay close enough
to be there in time.

I want to pay
attention to Michael
who is explaining the transfer
of fuel from tug to barge, but, distracted,
keep looking back,
girls, be careful!; the sky
over the river a marled
gray, the color of resentment;
the air sulfurous,
smell of rain or conflagration.

3

Wang-Wei, are you still waving good-bye?

Back home, I thought of his hut
wedged in the mountain
as we huddled in the basement,
the radio tracking thunderheads moving east,
flinging tornados
from its front like tops, and the lightning
like static made visible,
like a tapped light bulb with a loose connection.

He was a sap, I thought, young, though I read
his simple poems again
and again,
his hair growing white,
the figure of his friend diminishing
down the steep path
until a green-tinted mist obscured
them both.

4

All we have is the work, the words, yes?
In your Pound edition, his
signature: black ink,
not a moment's doubt. The Brilloed hair
flaring winglike
in the later photographs, the profile
that could cut stone
still, against the fact
of his aphasia, *mere* hesitancy?,
his cane tapping through a black-and-white
garden, his in any case
wordless halt; "I've made a botch
of it all . . ."

5

Why no matronymic
for the river? Why this Pound, this Wei, this Wright,
this gorgeous sound-beast
with war in its belly? But you see, Aleda,
this shy Ophelia on the verge
stepping from my shadow.
So young, she can be welcomed,
but the party spooks her. Commerce
between beauty and
honesty has slit her tongue.
Her hands are water.
She cannot speak for rescue.

6

The warning passed into watch
and the watch passed. I carried the girls
two flights back to sleep.
In the news next day: five dead,
though none in this country, none close,
the kind of death we have to stand.

Overall there has been more pleasure
though I thirst, still.

And know my own pain, barely.

When you go
you take the river in your poems,
a dragon-skinned current moving left to right
through the briefcase open in your lap.
You dip your hand.

Oh mirabilia!
The trees have thrown their arms to the ground
in the night, the sun gleams like a medal on a fresh uniform,
and we are flung here on another shore, alive!

III. Animal Discount

Bajo Cruces y Espadas

Translation: where we are. History, you
rotting face with wild plumage,
release me into this moment
and have done. Cortez

picks his teeth with an ivory needle
as the native is tortured and
waves curl in like crushed
glass. They were bluer

then, above the shore's blond beard
the white cries of gulls, mast
and compass, compass and
mast. And the march

through mountains, the bitchy elephants,
the endless hunger of insects.
I knelt to the stream,
a dark vein in the snow,

my mouth blind in alpine water. What
pageantry, the idiots say, what
emblems of the spirit!
I say the trench

smells of excrement and someone else's
fantasy. I say we learn bullet
and throw a tarp over God.
I say history's

a night spent mute and without fires,
dark tube greased by our own
fluids, long fall under stars,
crosses and swords.

Fable of the Knife

A happy knife left home seeking fortune. It met a man lifting weights. *Please sir,* it said, *May I have some of those weights, that I might build a house?* The man with the weights threw a barbell on the knife, bending it. The knife limped on until it came to a man at a political rally. *Please sir,* it asked the man, *What's going on?* The man picked up the knife and threw it into a tree. The knife trembled in the bark. At last the knife freed itself and labored down the street, until it came to a man humming to himself. *Please sir,* the knife said, *teach me to sing.* The man looked at the knife quizzically for a moment, then picked it up and drew a thin red line across his wrist with the knife's head. The knife twisted free and ran, blood seeping down its chin. After wiping itself in the grass, finally the knife booked a room at an inn, where it had a hearty repast of steak and potatoes. Later, in bed, the knife had time to reflect. *How strange,* it thought, *are the uses one is put to in this life. Surely my father, the cleaver, could have better prepared me . . .* And then fell fast asleep.

Animal Discount

Beginning is difficult, zygote
hesitation. Porch-level grackles
purr and click in the branches
like flywheels. That might do,
but are those cats serious,

planted at the tree's roots,
staring up with pink tongues?
Any question I can answer's
not worth—what? Flesh
and blood? A pound of feathers?

My nocturnal twin would like
a word here: *ash razor sank,
lip and tie, lip and tie.*
And you should hear when she's
drunk, a raving corpse!

How do we go on, knowing
there's an old woman puttering
in the kitchen below us, and
beneath that a basement full
of bony cats, and beneath

that the empire of worms,
beneath that a warming trend;
then the unbearable center
and the slow rise back into
form ... Listen, when you haggle

with God it's best to use your
green voice, and smack your wallet
right on the table, animal
discount showing, photograph
visible, dated, undeniable: you.

Objects in Mirror are Closer Than They Appear

As thumb is genius of the hand,
able to touch each other with rapidity
and fly back home to his isolate bungalow

before you can say fly, say finger say Mozart,
so can I maneuver two thousand pounds
looking backward. Where is childhood? I'm not

asking for the hell of it, I really
have paid to know. Twilight was so long, ground
so far from father's eyes, difficult

to get where all that memory's kept,
to just say *now,* and *this* and *this* and *this* . . .
But I do it. Because how else. Because once

all that drift of shadows and grass in summer,
Ronnie practicing drums after dinner,
bike in street, bright slivers

of an airplane crashed before we moved
there, found and kept in the box guarded by ballerina,
tart cousin smell, her hair shiny and black

as a telephone, breasts we compared
and both found wanting, the boys' awkward,
electric leers . . . What you have to watch is

you don't trust what you see in that mirror
to be far as seems, that you don't cut in front
and pull the tonnage of what's passed right through you.

Questionable Weather

The sky doesn't know what it wants to do—
blue mixes with white, hair of a fragile old woman.
One of the kids has planted a rubber ball
in with the geraniums, and the head of a worker

next door floats above the fence, covered by a skullcap
speckled with paint. Surely all the elements
of the earth converge in the smallest backyard,
where an average Joe just trying to get along

sips vodka in a lawn chair, and a dragonfly, most
exquisite green, zips through his vision like a biplane.
If the world, as those people who can take it
or leave it claim, is whole and perfect each moment,

what about those moments when speechless infants
die? A tough one, one that goes a long way to prove
faith has no common language. What I want to know is, do
those clouds mean rain? Shall I bring the cushions in?

Shore Report

All sand, all a gloss on memory
              walking in the dunes is forbidden
        the slim grass too fragile

a sun that fails to convince, green filtered
              that boy, his ropy limbs such ease
        ecological darts

now clears, humidity sucked halfway across
              Atlantic, gray haired and stubborn
        aluminum chairs, striped

come child not so far into the foam
              come child come child
        lotion, salt, flesh,

all sand, all a gloss on memory
              and the board found his head
        blood in rivulets

sea mixed, no body recovered at that depth
              horseshoe crabs, beached, broken helmets
        come child not so far

string tied to the gull's foot, so ache, heart
              salt pump and the wave curls
        poor man's kite

home now and the sand in secret grooves
              shiver in the cold spray, rub
        soap hates the hand

waves advance like rolls of film, kids smiling
            come child not so far
        shy sun new season

all sand, a gritty gloss on memory

Silk Robe

Green as that summer fly,
the quick one who looks like a flying emerald,
that green. Embroidered flowers
on the back, wide sleeves and front
panels; must have taken forever.
Light, you said, trying it on,
like nothing. And though you never
wear it, I'm glad it hangs
in your closet, thin and dark as a leaf.
Because my gift
for the beginning of love, meant
to be worn alone, nothing
underneath, and only flesh
touching silk, silk
touching flesh—the way your name
still feels in my mouth—
remains.

Restoration

The childless couple
pour their hearts into the old house
and weekend by weekend,
as the contractors follow the wife's pointed
finger, the chipped and rotten falls
away, and the new—stone and plank
cut and placed to look old—
rises. She knows her mind,
and the door will be red with robin's-egg-blue
frame; the goldfish pond a rectangle
cut in the earth six feet from the flagstone
walk leading to dunes; a slat fence
dividing her land from
the Atlantic. How hard they work! In an emerald green
jumpsuit she moves like a hummingbird
through house and yard, hovering here, then
there, while her husband, cool-
skinned, sporting khaki shorts and a full
mustache, carts tiles from one room to another,
a slightly bewildered curl
to his lip. Finally, it's finished!
The house is on the town's historic tour,
the DAR nails a tin shield beside the robin's-egg-
blue doorframe. Now they can breathe salt
air every weekend, together, away from the well-paid
stress of international law, interior
design ... In the upstairs
bedroom they draw lace curtains and switch
on a single yellow light. And make
love, thinking *Uhmmmmm, my house, just as
it was two hundred years ago, but better,
our whole lives ahead of us!*—as they move
upon each other, two creatures,
each half of one motion
older than the house, older than the town,

nearly as old as the moon and the sea,
that battered engine now boiling
and glistening in the freshly painted view
from their window.

Inversion

The will may bend light
rays, you may give me a thunderstorm
in a glass sphere; I just want a cup of coffee.
I just want a little break.

I hear enormous things are happening
in the lower latitudes, but not
as loudly as the mosquito who wants to live
in my ear like a vibrating needle.

Mural of pain, history, you would kill
for the saturated blue of
my lover's eyes when she rages
and the walls tense, and the lights flicker.

One day I woke up and said
to existence *I know you have me, but I as much
have you,* and went out in the rain,
and with the others hurried home.

Echo Off

This is rain from another century, this
clings to the downside of bare branches, this
gray chest full of swirling capes this
rain of gaslights and hitched up ruffles . . .

Do it, the parakeet says, adding her song
to tap water left running, or the nattering
of computer printout. But do what, I wonder?
We are each of us a hard task let go

in time. Our will is our own, all else belongs
and takes no pride in its belonging.
You see I care nothing for description, care
only, really, that I properly remove the stain

from Rimbaud's trousers. *Now* I've said it!
Once a thing is said, does it retire, does it?
Death is a video game (Phil said)—no matter how good
you are it *will* end. Lord, how profound.

Look, I don't want to keep you. You have your own
room, your own child, your own little night,
your own rain. And even if I stepped through this page
and embraced you I couldn't ease that longing.

IV. Thanksgiving Over the Water

*The wind has a voice coming over the waves,
and it is sadder than the end.*
—Stephen Crane

Invitation to the Dreamer

All night, my wife says, I keep moving—
I twitch, I revolve in the dark sheets,
I run on one leg like a dreaming dog.
But when I wake, what occupied hills,
what rocky coasts and bombed-out
buildings I've climbed; I don't remember.
The face in the bathroom mirror looks
vaguely familiar, though lined, crushed
and knocked off-center. Hello. Face
of an old friend come back to me
at great cost, bearing your heart-
breaking secret, spit it out. Don't stand
there, speechless, gaunt, imploring;
who needs a story to change a life
that can't be told? Say it, friend—
tell where you've been all night,
if not the whole at least the walking
bones. Don't let the silence stand
for answer, don't let your other self
believe the nothing day leads up
only to nothing night, and the star
lock, and the repetitious moon. Speak.

Thanksgiving Over the Water

Cry, child, for what is and what is coming.
Add your salt praise to the gifted water.
Cry long, until the walls are moved to sing.

This peace, which passes all understanding,
where is it? Can I take silence for an answer?
Cry for what is, child, and what is coming.

A wish might, but I wouldn't. Turning
from the ghost twins of grief and laughter
cry long, until the walls move, and sing.

In the book of waves the saints are drowning.
What are their cries to the faithless pastor?
Cry, child, for what is, and is coming.

Over the stone font and sea wall: muttering.
Words fall like rain on slate gray water.
Cry, cry until long walls are moved to sing.

In some beyond wind speaks. Here, nothing;
wave on wave. Time is the body's only lover.
Cry, child, for what is and what is coming.
Cry long, until the walls move and sing.

Lacrimae Patris

My friend has lost his father
and floats in a cold region: upstate
New York, so much blank ice between cities

and nothing over his head, nothing
between him and the next step,
what is it, crying it so deeply Sada

hears Utica in Boston, calls
and the electronic soothing
(how many thousand miles of human

warmth wrapped in frozen cable,
night on night!) does what it can, *You
have got to stop drinking and smoking*

so much, of course your eyes are bleeding!
All right. But then what? What if
I perfect this lousy machine, veins

clear as unwrapped syringes, muscles
pure and dense as young wood, then
what? Then the next poem and the next

thirteen-hour play by Brooks,
and the hand on my thigh again? Or light
on my hand in the strong sun of winter

break, Curaçao or the Keys? The next
page of the new genius of the
dead city? Or buffalo en flambe,

sea snake en croute, white trash salad?
I used to think London was a jerk,
but are we not episodes, only? Now even

the mirror delight of questions palls . . .
Oh woman, heart of my heart; sometimes I must
pound the dawn into my forehead.

Mermaid's Purse

The idea is to drift to the bottom and anchor the sticky horns to some stable object, then simply sway in the current while the embryo, rolled up inside like a crepe, develops. Then when the infant skate is ready the case splits open up a seam, and the fish wriggles out, unrolls and swims off. The idea is not to be held in the fist of a wave and slammed down on the shore, stillborn among the drying wrack and the fragments of star coral. I turn the case, now dried like old leather, over in my hand, then toss it back in the sea. It might have some small chance. Back at the blanket my oldest daughter pours wet sand on her sister's foot, and her sister screams. Peace between them is always fragile, always momentary. The two-year-old stutter steps wailing into her mother's arms, and I take her sister for a walk along the water line. There she makes a game of what is livelihood for the sandpiper, skipping along close to the water between waves, then running up to me as the next one comes in, just ahead of the foam. Her movements are at once delicate and awkward. Blond, blue-eyed, her mother's legs, she is pretty enough for me not to worry about the sorrow of that kind of rejection. Like all children she is still eternal, and often says *yesterday* when she means *tomorrow* . . . Looking down as she runs at her shadow running before her she slams into a fat man staring out at the waves with his hands on his hips. She cries and I pick her up and put her on my shoulders for diversion. She calms and we turn to walk back into the sun, toward our blanket. We are a tower of blue eyes. We are thirty-eight pounds of the future on top of a man happy to bear it, terrified by his happiness, walking on hard sand well away from the undertow.

All Saints

I praise the air, clear as an infant's will.
I praise the run and leap into the center

of so much color, the formic smell of decay
beginning. And the one leaf

always caught in my jacket collar . . .
Some guy works a chain saw a few streets away—

raw snore of the worm in the wood.
The present is only the ruled edge of the past;

if I extend my arm it is a finished thing.
And this falling the world does

every year gives back
both the boy and the death at once—

even now my old age strolls. I look down.
Shadow of a dead cricket etched on the sidewalk . . .

I wish I hadn't given up smoking, wish
I could stand on the wood porch, lean one hand

on the rail (a cold nail head in my palm),
and light up. Burn with the blue clarity of such sky.

Salt Marsh Cordgrass

Down the upper border
of phragmites and marsh elder,
on foot through black rush and salt
meadow hay of the high marsh,
      to the near water
zone and the lip of the estuary: cordgrass,
genius of the marsh, leaves
      speckled with salt, swaying its green.
The mud in its arms all summer
(roots and rhizomes holding the bank), it gives
us tiny white flowers in August,
      then falls,

decayed, and washes to the sea.
      And the leaves, eaten
alive by crab and insect, broken down by death
into detritus, a mixture
      of fine particles, food for fish, clam,
      and on down to microscopic
first links in the food chain: utterly useful
life, survivor of tides, breath-giver,
      deep unyielding matrix. . . .

The Starling Migration

Each morning they pass over
wiping their ragged scarf of cries
across the sky

and I am struck again by the miracle
of any voice,

even the blare of cat-fight
snarls in a drift of dead leaves,
even the crickets who sing the dry shadows.

       And the band marching
on distant fields, drums clumping
like some shaggy beast;

garbagemen who clatter their
    armor; squeal

of unseen tires; meaty bark
of a chained Lab, and the answer
from another yard—

all this should be worth praise
(he thought,
house quiet and the women asleep),

all this calling out
caught in the loop of time and sensation
(where
do they go, the starlings, do they know
a better here?),

each cry of travel and presence—

I give thanks, I lift up my eyes
to a sky
alive with fresh light and busy wings.

The Ocean All Day, All Night

If the ocean would just settle down
maybe the sandpipers could concentrate,
maybe I could figure out
what water's always on the verge of saying—

what it whispers when the wind's out of town,
what it screams like a lunatic
when the moon tilts, and the breakers
pound, white-knuckled, on the shore.

And if the ocean would stop testing its skin
like a nervous beast
I could reach into its belly
and pull out the secret of life,
finned and shimmering and undulant
in the sun.

Or if it would decide
yes, or *no,* instead of dissolving both;
if it would spell out any word
instead of endlessly jumbling
its alphabet of salt;
if it would step out of *The Kingdom
of Somewhere Between Life
and Death,* and be still—

then I could measure its intention
I could ask the hard question
I could offer my praise with a clear mind . . .

But no, the ocean stays restless as a man
troubled and stirred by his business
all day; turning first one way,
then another in his sleep all night.

The Moment When the Workers of the Night Pass by the Workers of the Day

Down at the salt marsh there is no pleading.
The sun itself begins as a seed in the cordgrass
nest, until its sudden birth spreads light
across the sea with the speed of burning cellophane,

walks inland, stepping window to window,
birdbath to gutter (light has a weightless
step), until even the dark soul of the first shift
turns in its sour sleep and wakens, the panic-

bars creak and a sluggish rope of men shakes
eight hours from their clothes, trading cracks
with the day-shift coming on with the smell of fresh
shirts and Aqua Velva, measuring their thirst and desire.

But it's across town the real money's made
these days, in buildings poured level by level,
thin slabs of Italian marble facing the treated
concrete, fifteen levels of spiral linked parking

below, as if the whole were screwed into the earth.
And the sudden hush of mahogany row, puce carpet
of deepest pile, the carved wooden doors
that once opened a sacred Hindu temple, each

as large as four large men, now block the CEO from non-
essential eyes. His windows are tinted gold, and when
the sun rises to his level it looks itself goldly
in the face, clouds drifting in the mirrored plaque

like fish. It may be I am reading this all wrong.
It may be the hard moment, moment when the workers
of the night pass by the workers of the day that renders
both illegible, and the pleading I see written there

is written in me. Perhaps, like stars and reasons
for murder, such faces are not friendly to explication,
are only what they appear—subterranean,
drained white and bitter as wild onions growing

under a flat stone, sockets for the male prongs
of television, dead-tired caves so full of one thing
after another there is no room for the slightest mystery.
Down at the salt marsh there is no pleading—

on foot through black rush and salt meadow hay
to the near water zone and the lip of the estuary,
looking down—a blue crab, motionless. He has lost
one claw. But human pity is less to him than the sun

now beginning to lean hard on his fierce back
and he sidles purposefully away, handlike, across
the shallow, as angled light throws shadows of small
rocks in his path, and he knows all the work ahead

but nothing of the hours hurtling from his body
which meet and join the hours hurtling from my body
toward the open sea. Dawn . . . Who are we always waving to?
Who flicks the light, strokes our faces, hurries on?

About the Author

JEFFREY SKINNER was born in 1949 in Buffalo, New York. He received his B.A. from Rollins College in Florida and his M.F.A. in Writing from Columbia University. His poems have appeared in *The Atlantic*, *The Nation*, *The New Yorker*, *Paris Review*, and many other magazines. His previous books are *Late Stars* and *A Guide to Forgetting*, which was chosen by Tess Gallagher for the 1987 National Poetry Series. He is Associate Professor of English at the University of Louisville.

Pitt Poetry Series
Ed Ochester, General Editor

Claribel Alegría, *Flowers from the Volcano*
Claribel Alegría, *Woman of the River*
Debra Allbery, *Walking Distance*
Maggie Anderson, *Cold Comfort*
Maggie Anderson, *A Space Filled with Moving*
Robin Becker, *Giacometti's Dog*
Siv Cedering, *Letters from the Floating World*
Lorna Dee Cervantes, *Emplumada*
Robert Coles, *A Festering Sweetness: Poems of American People*
Nancy Vieira Couto, *The Face in the Water*
Kate Daniels, *The Niobe Poems*
Kate Daniels, *The White Wave*
Toi Derricotte, *Captivity*
Sharon Doubiago, *South America Mi Hija*
Stuart Dybek, *Brass Knuckles*
Odysseus Elytis, *The Axion Esti*
Jane Flanders, *Timepiece*
Gary Gildner, *Blue Like the Heavens: New & Selected Poems*
Elton Glaser, *Color Photographs of the Ruins*
Barbara Helfgott Hyett, *In Evidence: Poems of the Liberation of Nazi Concentration Camps*
David Huddle, *Paper Boy*
Lawrence Joseph, *Curriculum Vitae*
Lawrence Joseph, *Shouting at No One*
Julia Kasdorf, *Sleeping Preacher*
Etheridge Knight, *The Essential Etheridge Knight*
Bill Knott, *Poems: 1963–1988*
Ted Kooser, *One World at a Time*
Ted Kooser, *Sure Signs: New and Selected Poems*
Larry Levis, *The Widening Spell of the Leaves*
Larry Levis, *Winter Stars*
Larry Levis, *Wrecking Crew*
Irene McKinney, *Six O'Clock Mine Report*
Archibald MacLeish, *The Great American Fourth of July Parade*
Peter Meinke, *Liquid Paper: New and Selected Poems*
Peter Meinke, *Night Watch on the Chesapeake*
Carol Muske, *Applause*
Carol Muske, *Wyndmere*
Leonard Nathan, *Carrying On: New & Selected Poems*
Sharon Olds, *Satan Says*
Alicia Suskin Ostriker, *Green Age*

Alicia Suskin Ostriker, *The Imaginary Lover*
Greg Pape, *Black Branches*
Greg Pape, *Storm Pattern*
Kathleen Peirce, *Mercy*
David Rivard, *Torque*
Liz Rosenberg, *The Fire Music*
Maxine Scates, *Toluca Street*
Richard Shelton, *Selected Poems, 1969–1981*
Betsy Sholl, *The Red Line*
Peggy Shumaker, *The Circle of Totems*
Jeffrey Skinner, *The Company of Heaven*
Gary Soto, *Black Hair*
Gary Soto, *The Elements of San Joaquin*
Gary Soto, *The Tale of Sunlight*
Gary Soto, *Where Sparrows Work Hard*
Leslie Ullman, *Dreams by No One's Daughter*
Constance Urdang, *Alternative Lives*
Ronald Wallace, *The Makings of Happiness*
Ronald Wallace, *People and Dog in the Sun*
Belle Waring, *Refuge*
Michael S. Weaver, *My Father's Geography*
Robley Wilson, *Kingdoms of the Ordinary*
Robley Wilson, *A Pleasure Tree*
David Wojahn, *Glassworks*
David Wojahn, *Mystery Train*
Paul Zimmer, *Family Reunion: Selected and New Poems*